Just Write

Creativity and Craft in Writing

Book 2

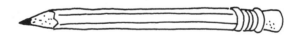

Alexandra S. Bigelow • Elsie S. Wilmerding

EDUCATORS PUBLISHING SERVICE
Cambridge and Toronto

Acknowledgments

Many thanks to the third-grade students at the
Brimmer and May School for all their editing help with *Just Write* Book 2,
our second writing workbook.

Design: Persis Barron Levy
Typesetting: Karen Lomigora

Printed in Benton Harbor, MI, in May 2012
ISBN 978-0-8388-2627-0

12 13 14 15 16 PPG 16 15 14 13 12

Contents

Introduction

This book was written for your enjoyment. Have fun discovering different ways to write! Before you begin any exercise, please take the time to flip through the entire book. Notice some of the things you will be learning about, such as how to write an interesting story, how to write conversation, and how to use more interesting words.

Now take a minute to turn to the back of the book. Look at page 157 and notice the resource materials that will be helpful at different times as you progress through the writing exercises in the book. There are webs to help you organize your thoughts, content and editing checklists to help make your story the best that it can be, and a list of synonyms to help you use a variety of words.

Don't be afraid to experiment with your writing. Practice using the different maps and strategies. And just write! This will help you to learn the methods that are best for you.

Chapter 1
Working with Sentences

Good sentences build good paragraphs and stories. You already know a lot about sentences. You know that sentences express a complete thought. You also know that sentences begin with a capital letter and end with punctuation. You know that a sentence can end with a period, a question mark, or an exclamation mark. But do you know what the two main parts of a sentence are called? There are a lot of interesting things to learn about sentences!

Reviewing Capitals and Basic Punctuation

Before we begin to talk about sentences, it is important to review capitals and basic punctuation. All sentences begin with a capital letter and end with punctuation.

Capitals

Always use a capital letter at the beginning of a sentence. This helps your readers see where a new sentence begins.

Examples

    1. **A**ll the cars stopped to let the dog cross the road.

    2. **H**e looked both ways and scampered to the other side.

    3. **W**e were very relieved.

✎ Practice

Rewrite these sentences with a capital letter at the beginning.

1. we had fun on the merry-go-round.

_____

2. the lake was very cold.

_____

3. maria slipped on a banana peel.

_____

4. that food smells very good.

_____

5. did they make you laugh?

_____

Basic Punctuation

Use a **period** at the end of a sentence that makes a statement.

Use a **question mark** at the end of a sentence that asks a question.

Use an **exclamation mark** at the end of a sentence to express a strong feeling.

These different types of punctuation help your reader see where one sentence ends and another begins. They also help your reader understand your story by making it easier to see the feelings in your sentences.

Here are three example sentences. Notice how each one begins with a capital letter and ends with punctuation: a period, a question mark, or an exclamation mark.

Statement: Josh and his uncle like to walk through the woods.

Question: Where did Regina get her ideas for her story?

Strong feeling: Hey, watch out for that spider!

✏ Practice

Remember, when you write a sentence:

- Begin it with a capital letter.
- End it with punctuation.

Rewrite these sentences with a capital letter at the beginning and the correct punctuation at the end.

1. have you ever watched a bird take a bath

_____

_____

2. when we left the house the sun was shining

_____

_____

3. you look terrific

_____

_____

At the beginning of each sentence, cross out the lowercase letter and write a capital letter. Then put the correct punctuation mark at the end. The first one is done for you.

1. ~~d~~D̸o you have time to bake a cake this afternoon ?

2. the teacher asked the class to stand and sing a song

3. ooh, what a scary movie

4. be careful, that pan is really hot

5. when is your grandmother coming for a visit

6. i can't believe what I am seeing

7. rico has two brothers and one sister

8. what are you looking for

Other Uses for Capitals

Capital letters are not just for the beginning of a sentence. Sometimes you need to use them in the middle of a sentence too. Use capitals for names of people and places.

Example: **T**ahlia and **S**tanley went to **N**ew **J**ersey.

• Practice

Cross out the lowercase letters and write in capital letters where they are needed. Don't forget punctuation marks.

1. cleveland is a fun city

2. does mr. moss play music

3. california and alaska are huge states

4. yesterday emma turned seven years old

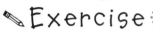

Exercise

Cross out the lowercase letters and write in capital letters where they are needed. Don't forget punctuation marks.

patrick and lila live in dallas, texas they are packing their bags to go

on a long trip with their uncle rob he has a really comfortable van with

sleeping cots, a little kitchen, and a tiny bathroom they are plan-

ning to leave dallas and drive east to jackson mis-

sissippi, where they will stay and visit cousins for

three days then they will climb back into the van

and go on to birmingham, alabama where they will

spend a week with uncle rob's son, jessie he is five years older than

patrick and lila, but the three of them always have a good time together.

Making Corrections

You already know that you must capitalize the names of people and places, and you know to use a capital letter at the beginning of a sentence and punctuation at the end. When you're writing, you may forget to use a capital letter or put punctuation at the end of a sentence. Sometimes it's more important to get the idea down on paper than it is to worry about grammar rules. That's okay, but you have to go back later to make corrections.

✎ Exercise

Read the following paragraph and see if you can find all the corrections that are needed. There are words that need capital letters and sentences that need proper punctuation. Make your corrections. When you are finished, reread the paragraph to make sure you didn't miss anything.

wow, did you see those beautiful tall ships, in the boston harbor last

year we had friends who came all the way from florida to see them eliza

brought her camera and took some amazing pictures did you get a

chance to see them yet

What Is a Sentence?

A sentence is a complete thought. A sentence must have two basic parts: a **subject** and a **predicate.** The subject of the sentence is a **noun:** a person, place, thing, or idea. The predicate describes what the subject is doing and must include a **verb.**

✎ Practice

Read the following sentences and answer the questions.

1. The turtle waddles.

   The turtle is the ___subject._____

   Waddles is the ___predicate._____

2. Ben will call.

   Will call is the _____

   Ben is the _____

3. The teacher asked questions.

   The teacher is the _____

   Asked questions is the _____

✎ Exercise

Write three simple sentences of your own.

1. _____

2. _____

3. _____

Now go back and (circle) the subjects and <u>underline</u> the predicates.

Working with Subjects and Predicates

You know that sentences have to have a subject. The subject is a noun (a person, place, thing, or idea) that does the action.

Here are some examples of subjects in sentences.

The subjects are underlined.

The white cat jumped away.

The parking lot was full of cats and dogs.

The fur on my cat feels very soft.

My cat has beautiful eyes.

✎ Practice

Here are some sentences that do not have subjects. What are these sentences about? Add a subject to each one.

1. _____ lives in our neighborhood.

2. My _____ takes the bus to work every day.

3. _____ stopped suddenly because a dog was on the road.

4. _____ prevented me from arriving on time.

5. _____ waved goodbye as I drove away.

6. _____ were grazing in the field next door.

7. _____ and _____ will come to the party.

You also know that sentences have to have a predicate. The predicate is a phrase that tells what the subject is doing. The predicate has to include a verb.

Here are some examples of predicates in sentences. The predicates are underlined, and the verbs are underlined twice.

The beautiful lion <u>sleeps on the warm rock</u>.

We <u>saw a lion last year</u>.

She <u>questioned my story</u>.

He <u>cried and stomped his foot with anger</u>.

✎ Practice

Here are some sentences that need verbs added for the predicate to be complete. Add a verb to each sentence to complete the predicate and tell what the subject is doing.

1. We _____ up on the lion.

2. My dad _____ baseball with me every night.

3. The chicken coop _____ so horrible that I have to hold my nose.

4. Jacob's father _____ is a policeman.

5. Michael _____ amazing pictures for his stories.

Sometimes the verb in the predicate does not show action; it acts as a "being verb." This kind of verb helps to join parts of the sentence. Here are a few examples:

Peggy <u>is</u> a dog.

I <u>am</u> a student at this school.

She <u>was</u> sick yesterday.

Make 5 more simple sentences using some of the underlined verbs above. Write some sentences with a predicate that shows action and some sentences with a "being verb" in the predicate. Remember that every sentence begins with a capital letter and ends with a period, a question mark, or exclamation mark.

1. _____

2. _____

3. _____

4. _____

5. _____

Now go back and (circle) the subjects and <u>underline</u> the predicates.

Complete Sentences and Fragments

Remember: every sentence needs a subject and a verb! If a sentence is missing the subject or the predicate, it is incomplete. Incomplete sentences are called **fragments** and can be frustrating to your reader.

• Practice

Read the following examples. Identify a complete sentence by putting a check on the line at the end. Put an X on the lines at the end of fragments (incomplete sentences).

1. Adam lost his little pet toad. ___

2. The shiny castle in the sun. ___

3. Waiting to ride the scooter. ___

4. Ms. Hufflepop floated around the lake on a raft. ___

5. And walked up the heavy, stone steps. ___

6. Mr. Snodweb loves to work in his vegetable garden. ___

7. The old, wobbly bridge that goes over the stream. ___

8. Something happened that made him scream. ___

9. Running beyond the fence is off limits. ___

10. Petunia and her brother Pedro spent their money on a pineapple. ___

11. If the spooky ghost jumps through the door. ___

12. I wish I could change these stuffed animals into real animals. ___

Here are some sentence fragments. In each, either the subject or the verb is missing. Turn each one into a complete and interesting sentence. The first two have been done for you. Don't forget capitals and correct punctuation!

1. plan to go the Halloween party

Jim and Jessie plan to go to the Halloween party.

2. tickled my stomach

While I was standing on my head, my sister tickled my stomach.

3. dove into the crashing wave

_____

4. the tiny baby

_____

5. learned how to read

_____

6. in the store

_____

7. the frog in the pond

_____

Write four complete sentences. If you wish, you may use the two lists at the bottom of the page for ideas. When you have finished, read each one carefully. Make sure your sentences have both a subject and a predicate. Remember to check for punctuation.

1. _____

2. _____

3. _____

4. _____

Subjects

the old man next door

the playground

Sally and Jimmy

his computer

Peggy, my dog,

Predicates

jumped over the wall

read the story

laughed out loud

exploded into pieces

questioned my answer

Now go back and circle the subject in each sentence and underline the predicate in each sentence.

Exercise 3

Write five complete sentences. Make sure that you have a subject and a predicate. Exchange papers with a friend and ask him or her to circle the subject and underline the predicate in each of your sentences.

1. _____

   _____

2. _____

   _____

3. _____

   _____

4. _____

   _____

5. _____

   _____

Now get your paper back from your friend and check to make sure they have circled each subject and underlined each predicate.

Working with Describing Words

Adjectives

You can make your sentences more interesting by using describing words. There are different kinds of describing words. **Adjectives** are words that describe nouns. Adjectives can tell what color something is, how big or small it is, or give other details of how it feels, looks, tastes, or sounds.

Think of at least five adjectives that you could use to describe yourself.

_____   _____

_____   _____

_____   _____

_____   _____

•Practice

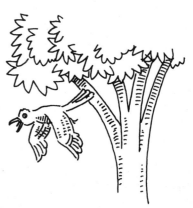

Underline the describing words in these sentences.

1. My dad has many colorful ties.

2. A huge bird flew out of the elm tree.

3. That tall girl is a fast runner.

4. The bald man got cold because he had lost his warm, fuzzy hat.

5. His delicious ice cream melted in the hot car.

✎ Exercise 1

Now it is your turn. Fill in the blanks with describing words.

1. The _____ children came home late.

2. My _____ dog ate our _____ dessert off the table.

3. This has been a _____, _____ winter.

4. Would you bring me your _____, _____ jacket?

5. The _____ story made all the _____ kids laugh.

✎ Exercise 2

With a partner, think of four adjectives for each of the nouns listed below. Pick the two you like the best and fill in the blanks.

1. _____, _____ shoes

2. _____, _____ monsters

3. the _____, _____ snake

4. the _____, _____ mail carrier

5. the _____, _____ moth

6. the _____ and _____ carpenter

7. the _____, _____ goblin

With your partner, write a short paragraph using at least six adjectives. Your paragraph should have at least three sentences. You can write about one of the items from Exercise 2, or you can think of something completely different to write about.

_____

_____

_____

_____

_____

_____

_____

_____

_____

_____

_____

_____

Adverbs

You can also use special describing words to make the verbs you choose more interesting. **Adverbs** are words that describe verbs. Adverbs describe how something is done. Most adverbs end in *ly*. Some common adverbs are *slowly, quickly, easily*, and *softly*.

•Practice

<u>Underline</u> the adverbs in the sentences below. Remember: adverbs are words that describe *how*.

1. The squirrel chattered loudly in the tree.

2. The train slowly pulled into the station.

3. Eric carefully finished his homework.

4. We quickly cleaned up our mess.

Now, it is your turn to fill in the blanks with adverbs, words that describe how. You may use the words below or you can think of your own. Try not to use the same word twice!

1. Nat tiptoed _____ into the bedroom so he would not wake up his brother.

2. The dog barked _____ in the backyard.

3. The alligator crawled _____ out of the water.

4. Leah _____ opened her present.

5. Erik _____ skateboarded down the street.

silently   loudly

slowly   completely

carefully   quickly

quietly   wildly

smoothly   softly

Writing Interesting Sentences

Now you have all the tools you need to write interesting sentences.

First choose a subject. (Circle) one of the subjects below that you'd like to write about, or come up with your own:

> The snake
>
> A bike
>
> The storm

Now add interesting details about the subject. Use the questions below to help.

Did what? _____

Where? _____

When? _____

Why? _____

Now write one sentence that uses all the details.

_____

_____

_____

_____

✎ Practice

Again, choose a subject. (Circle) the subject that you choose.

My baby-sitter

A spider

The noise

Now add interesting details about the subject using the questions below to help.

Did what? _____

Where? _____

When? _____

Why? _____

Now write one sentence that uses all the details.

_____

_____

_____

_____

This exercise will help you expand your sentences by explaining *why*.

Look at this example:

> I rinse my dog off with fresh water every time he swims in the ocean.

> I rinse my dog off with fresh water every time he swims in the ocean **because the salt makes him itch.**

Expand these sentences by choosing a, b, or c to explain *why*. Notice how the words *because, so,* and *to* help. Circle the best choice.

1. I water the plants every week

    a. because they are wet.

    b. so they won't dry out.

    c. because I love to experiment.

2. I always walk my dog on a leash

    a. because it is cold outside.

    b. to show off to the neighbors.

    c. because our town has a leash law.

3. I sat down on the step

    a. because I was tired.

    b. to put my bike in the garage.

    c. so mom can go to the market.

4. I make breakfast for my family on Sundays

    a. so it will be a sunny day.

    b. because I love to cook.

    c. to get better at soccer.

1. Write an interesting sentence telling *what* the hamster did and *where* he did it.

My hamster _____

_____

_____

_____

2. Write an interesting sentence telling *what* the adventure was, *where* it happened, and *when*.

The adventure _____

_____

_____

_____

3. Write an interesting sentence telling *what* the alien did, *where* he did it, and *why*.

The alien _____

_____

_____

_____

Rewrite the following sentences and add details by answering the question provided at the end of the sentence.

1. My family went on vacation. (when)

My family went on vacation last week.

2. I ran home from school. (why)

_____

3. I fell off my bike. (when)

_____

4. I put my homework away. (where)

_____

Combining
Your Sentences

Your reader will be more interested in your writing if it has a lot of variety. It is good to use some short sentences and some long sentences. An easy way to make a long sentence is to combine two short sentences with a connecting word.

Here are some words that you can use to combine your sentences:

but	and	since
or	so	because

✎ Practice

Choose the best word from page 24 to combine the two sentences below into one longer sentence. Use each word only once.

1. I wanted to go to the movies with my friends. Mom needed me to watch my sister.

_____

2. We had to hurry home. There was a sudden rainstorm.

_____

3. We can go to the seashore. We can go to the park.

_____

4. We had to end our baseball game. It got too dark to play.

_____

5. My sister, Reni, loves gymnastics. She also likes rock climbing.

_____

6. It was too cold to sleep in the tent. We went back to the camp.

_____

Choose the best word from page 27 to connect the two sentences into one interest-ing sentence. Use each word from the list only once.

1. This year I learned to kick a soccer ball. I also learned to throw a soccer ball.

_____

_____

_____

2. The movie was very funny. I was so tired I fell asleep before it was over.

_____

_____

3. I have to go home. My aunt needs me to help set up for my cousin's birthday party.

_____

_____

4. My new puppy made a mess on the floor. I had to clean it up.

_____

_____

5. Jeb missed the test on Friday. He was sick.

_____

_____

and

so

but

since

because

Sentence Checklist

You can use this checklist when you are reading through your sentences to help make sure they are complete and correct.

When you reread your sentences from pages 26–27:

☐ Does each sentence express a complete thought?

☐ Does each sentence begin with a capital letter and end with a punctuation mark?

☐ Did you include interesting details about your subject?

☐ Did you use adjectives and adverbs?

☐ Is your handwriting clear and easy to read?

Chapter 2
Working with Paragraphs

Now that you have all the tools you need to write interesting sentences, it's time to work on combining those sentences into interesting paragraphs.

What Is a Paragraph?

A **paragraph** is a group of at least three or four sentences that are related to one main idea. A paragraph needs a **topic sentence.** A topic sentence gives the reader the main idea of the paragraph. Read the following paragraph and see if you can find the topic sentence.

> Henry is nervous about moving from Minnesota to Nebraska. Up until now, he has lived in the city. Many of his friends live nearby, and they have fun playing in the neighboring park on Saturday afternoons. His new house will be on a farm, and his Dad is going to have cows, sheep, and maybe some horses. Although Henry loves animals, it will be very different living in the country. He likes school now, but he is worried about what his new school will be like.

<u>Underline</u> the topic sentence, and write what you think is the main idea of the paragraph.

_____

_____

Do you notice something special about the first line of a paragraph? The beginning of the paragraph is **indented.** Indenting is a way to show the beginning of a new paragraph. When you indent, you begin the first sentence of a paragraph with about two fingers' width of space from the left side of your paper. You can see an example in the drawing below:

• Practice

Read the following paragraph, and see if you can find the topic sentence.

The giant spider crab is found deep in the water off the coast of Japan. Unlike the crabs we can buy in the store here, these Japanese crabs are really huge! Generally they are from eight to fifteen feet wide. Giant spider crabs are so big and heavy that the Japanese fishermen use special traps to catch them and tow them back to shore. Even though the giant crabs' legs are long and spider-like, they contain several pounds of delicious meat. The meat of the giant spider crab is so popular that it is shipped to many other countries for people to eat.

Underline the topic sentence, and write what you think is the main idea of the paragraph.

_____

_____

_____

_____

Don't be tricked! The topic sentence is not always found in the beginning. Read the following paragraph and notice where the topic sentence is.

Almost every morning Jimmy shoots a few hoops before breakfast. At school, he plays kickball during recess. After school, he often plays catch with his friends. On Saturdays, his baseball team usually has a game. <u>Jimmy loves sports.</u>

Now read this paragraph and <u>underline</u> the topic sentence.

James Cook, an early explorer of the Pacific, was a very fine captain, but he also cared for his crew. One of his biggest worries was that his men would get sick. He was anxious to prevent his crew from getting scurvy, a disease that had killed many sailors on earlier voyages. He made his men eat enormous amounts of onions, salt, and oatmeal. He cooked them coconut milk and even prepared meals from grasses from the tropics. His crew stayed healthy. Captain Cook proved that eating certain foods could prevent disease.

✎ Exercise 2

In the exercise below, you will see that each paragraph needs a topic sentence. At the end of each selection, choose the best topic sentence and write it on the line at the top. The first one has been done for you.

1. __There are many different styles of living.__

    Many people live in high apartment buildings. My uncle lives on a boat all year long. My friend lives in a trailer and is always traveling to new places.

    a. Jessica lives in a log cabin by a lake in New Hampshire.

    b. My cousin's apartment in New York is on the twenty-eighth floor.

    c. There are many different styles of living.

2. _____

    In Florida, pelicans continually hover near the water and dive for fish. Herons can also be seen quietly fishing along the banks. The Ibis is another lovely, long legged bird living along the water down there.

    a. Herons can be nasty if they feel threatened.

    b. There are many beautiful birds in Florida.

    c. Florida is a fun place to go.

3. _____

    Aunt Matilda knits me sweaters and long fuzzy scarves. She goes skating with my two brothers every Saturday. Aunt Matilda and my cousins often dress up and perform plays.

    a. Aunt Matilda is my mother's sister.

    b. My Aunt Matilda is talented and fun to be with.

    c. Aunt Matilda is a good athlete.

4. _____

   The Atlantic salmon's life begins in a freshwater river as a tiny egg. Its first year as a baby fish, or a fry, is spent in the river. Then its incredible journey begins. It travels to the ocean where it spends two or three years. In the spring, if the water is high enough, the salmon works back to the river where it was born. It is then a full-grown salmon ready to lay eggs of its own.

   a. The salmon is a difficult fish to catch.

   b. The salmon has a remarkable life.

   c. Fish can be farmed in the ocean.

5. _____

   Mica and Holly love to wear shorts and sandals. Kelly has studs and fringes on her jacket. Jeff and Willy like wearing cowboy boots. Mrs. Nolan wears her running clothes all the time. Mr. Jacobs always wears his favorite hat, and my mom likes to wear her work clothes, even on Sundays.

   a. Everyone has different tastes in clothing.

   b. Mom goes to work every day but Sunday.

   c. Mrs. Nolan will run the marathon this year.

✎ Exercise 3

In the exercises below, the supporting details are given. It is your job to write a topic sentence on the line above each group of sentences. The first one is done for you.

1. _Mara can speak many languages._

   Her dad is from Vietnam, so Mara can speak Vietnamese. Mara lives in Montreal, and she can speak French, too. Mara likes to play with two friends from Mexico, and they teach her Spanish words.

2. _____

   Two summers ago, my big brother Jeff did some volunteer work at a day camp in the city. Last summer, he worked painting houses to earn money for college. This is his last summer before college, and he plans to work as a tutor in a summer school.

3. _____

   My teacher, Mrs. Curly, has shown us fun science experiments. Last week in science class, we searched for bugs and worms in the field in back of the school. Mrs. Curly also teaches us amazing things about the sun and stars.

4. _____

   The tiger is an endangered animal. The tortoise is also endangered. I just learned that the black rhinoceros is an endangered animal, too.

Supporting Sentences

To make your paragraph complete, you need to explain your topic sentence. The sentences that you write to explain your topic sentence are called **supporting sentences.**

Read this sentence. Do you feel like it gives you the information that you need?

It is important to wear a life jacket when you go out in a boat.

Now read the paragraph below. Three supporting sentences were added to explain the first sentence. There is more information about the topic, which makes it much more interesting.

It is important to wear a life jacket when you go out in a boat. Even if you are a good swimmer, it can be helpful. If the boat tips over, you could be far from land and have to tread water for a long time before someone rescues you. Also, you could hurt yourself when you tip over, and the life jacket could keep you afloat even if you are not able to swim.

✎ Practice

Here is a sentence for you to expand with details. Add two or three supporting sentences to give more meaning and understanding of the topic. Have fun and be as creative as you want.

The field trip was fun._____

_____

_____

_____

Work with a partner to expand these paragraphs with supporting sentences. Add two or three sentences to give more meaning and understanding to the topic. Have fun!

1. The coach had the team meet in a huddle at halftime. _____

_____

_____

_____

_____

2. I told my little brother to stay out of my room. _____

_____

_____

_____

_____

_____

The topic sentence has been given. Add at least two supporting sentences.

1. I am so excited because next week is my birthday. _____

_____

_____

_____

2. Sasha and I always have a good time when we go to the movies. _____

_____

_____

_____

3. It was incredible to stand next to an elephant! _____

_____

_____

_____

✎ Exercise 3

Now answer the question *why*. Write at least two detailed supporting sentences.

1. My friend Zack is fun to visit because _____

_____

_____

_____

_____

2. Third grade is different from last year because _____

_____

_____

_____

_____

3. Diana's party was so much fun! _____

_____

_____

_____

_____

Answer the questions *how, what,* or *why* to fill in details for each paragraph.

1. When we went to the pond yesterday, we saw a lot of interesting creatures.

_____

_____

_____

_____

2. There are several things that I can do well._____

_____

_____

_____

3. I had to work hard to learn how to _____

_____

_____

_____

_____

Now you know that a complete paragraph needs a topic sentence and supporting details. Read each short paragraph and decide if it is complete or not. Put a check next to the complete ones and an X next to the ones that need more supporting details.

1. My dad found out that his new car had rolled down the driveway and crashed into a telephone pole. The whole back fender and the rear lights need to be replaced. My mom had forgotten to put on the brake, but luckily no one was hurt. _____

2. My vacation was lots of fun. Hopefully we can go back to the same place next year. It was pretty. My sister loved it too because she made new friends. _____

3. Our house is full of different kinds of gloves. My mom has gardening gloves, some are rubbery and some are leather. My dad has work gloves mostly for the outside. Everyone has warm, lined gloves for the winter. Jeff and Brad, my brothers, always leave their hockey gloves around the house, and my sister seems to be always missing a mitten. _____

4. Janna's bed is always unmade. There are old potato chip bags lying on the floor with her toys and stuffed animals. That nice desk is covered with papers and tapes, and her clothes are everywhere. You can't even find the rug! _____

5. Uncle Pete has a huge chicken farm in Kansas. It is fun to visit. _____

Writing Your Own Paragraphs

You now have all the tools you need to write interesting, complete paragraphs. You know how to combine subjects and predicates into sentences and how to add details to make them interesting. You know how to join two shorter sentences to make one long one. You know how to write a topic sentence and add supporting sentences to make a complete paragraph. Look at the following paragraph and see how it all works together.

The topic of this paragraph is *The Playground at School.*

We have a wonderful playground at our school. There is a huge swing set and a big jungle gym. The jungle gym has ropes to climb on and there is also a slide. The sandbox is on one side. Ten or twelve people can play in there at once. My friends and I sit there and pretend that we are cooking for guests in a fancy restaurant. There are also tires to swing on, huge tubes to climb through, and a balance beam to practice on. Some kids like to play basketball or soccer, and others just like to talk. Everyone loves the new playground.

Now go back and (circle) the topic sentence. <u>Underline</u> the supporting details about the playground.

• Practice

Choose a topic from the list below. (Circle) it. Think about some good supporting details that would fit with your topic and write them on the lines. They do not need to be complete sentences.

Topics

a special friend

my favorite sport

something I like to do

Details:

_____

_____

_____

_____

_____

_____

Now write a complete paragraph using the topic and details from the page before. Don't forget to write a topic sentence and to use capital letters and punctuation where you need them. Also, think about where you can use joining words to connect your supporting details. Here are some good joining words: *and, also, but, because.*

_____

_____

_____

_____

_____

_____

_____

_____

_____

_____

In the space below, draw a picture to go along with your paragraph.

Something Important to Me

Now it's time for you to write a paragraph about something important to you. Read this short model first.

> My neighbor, Mrs. Bremmin, is very important to me. She lets me help her pick vegetables from her garden. Sometimes I play with my friend in her barn, and last month Mrs. Bremmin let me feed one of her newborn calves with a bottle. That was so much fun. She is so kind and gentle, and she has taught me a lot about growing things and taking care of animals.

Here are some possible choices for your topic, or you can choose your own:

- playing with a special friend
- a hobby, for example: basketball, collecting stickers, playing the piano, or something else
- my favorite game to play at recess

- good art supplies
- my favorite sport
- my favorite videogame
- my favorite book

What is your topic?

_____

List at least five details about your topic. They do not need to be complete sentences.

_____   _____

_____   _____

_____   _____

Write your paragraph below. Don't forget to:

- have a topic sentence

- have supporting details

- indent the first line

- start each new sentence with a capital letter and end it with the correct punctuation mark

Something Important to Me

_____

_____

_____

_____

_____

_____

_____

_____

Ending a Paragraph

There is one more important part to a complete paragraph. The last sentence should pull a paragraph together and summarize what you have been trying to say. Sometimes it repeats the topic sentence in a new way. This final sentence is called the **conclusion.**

Here is an example of a short paragraph with a conclusion. The conclusion is underlined.

This week has been a difficult one. I forgot to do my homework again, so Mr. Tidbits kept me in from recess for the third time. My Mom's car broke down. Now, she isn't able to go to the grocery store. We have been eating pizza for a week. I thought I could never get sick of pizza, but I don't think I ever want to eat it again! Lastly, my older brother is looking for a job, so he has no time to play soccer with me. <u>I really hope next week will be a better one!</u>

✎ Practice

Write a conclusion for the following paragraph.

I am feeling nervous and jumpy because tomorrow I will start my new school. My family moved, so I can't stay at my old school. I know only one kid in our new town, and he isn't in my class. My old school was near my house, but I have to ride a bus for twenty minutes to get to the new school. My dad says that I might have homework every night.

_____

_____

_____

Exercise 1

Finish these paragraphs with good concluding sentences.

Jimmy and Mike are similar in several ways. They are both nine years old and they are fourth graders. Both boys live on Chester Street, and they go to basketball practice together every Saturday. Jimmy has a one-year-old sister, and Mike has a little brother. Both Jimmy and Mike love to make silly faces to make the babies laugh.

_____

_____

_____

South Texas has different wildlife than where I live in New England. Scissor-tailed flycatchers are pretty birds with long, streaming tails. The roadrunner and the curlew are interesting, long-billed birds. We also spotted a coyote and a javelina, which is like a giant rat with two big tusks.

_____

_____

_____

Write a topic sentence (T.S.) and a concluding sentence (C.S.) for these supporting sentences.

1. **T.S.** _____

   Brush your teeth well and wash your face.

   Carefully comb your hair.

   Pick out your clothes and get dressed.

   Be sure to make your bed.

   Always eat a good breakfast.

   C.S. _____

2. **T.S.** _____

   Squirrels are tree dwellers.

   Beavers build lodges with sticks and mud.

   Bears hibernate in dens for the winter.

   Rabbits live in the woods, fields, and the desert.

   Gophers burrow in tunnels underground.

   C.S. _____

3. **T.S.** _____

   First check the weather forecast.

   Be sure to wear a sturdy pair of shoes.

   Pack a lunch, snacks, and plenty of water in a backpack.

   Layer clothes to prepare for temperature changes.

   Bring a compass and a watch.

   Always wear a hat with a brim.

   C.S. _____

How-To Paragraphs

When you write a paragraph about how to do something, you have to be sure that it is in the correct sequence. It helps to make a list of things you want to include and then put them in the correct order before you begin to write. Here is a list of words that can help you put the steps in the right order:

first

second

third

then

next

after

last

after

now

before

later

after a while

finally

when

• Practice

Look at the description below on how to sprout seeds. The first thing in the description is a list of what is needed to do the project.

How to Sprout Seeds

Materials Needed:

potting soil

small containers

seeds

misting bottle

clear plastic wrap

bottom-watering trays

labels

Number these steps to planting seeds in order:

_____ When seeds are covered spray lightly with mister.

_____ Finally, water the potting soil from the bottom tray.

_____ Second, evenly scatter seeds about 1 inch apart.

_____ First, fill containers with potting soil about a $\frac{1}{2}$ inch from top.

_____ After spraying, label and cover the containers with clear wrap.

_____ Then lightly cover seeds with soil.

Notice the words that help you to put steps in correct order. Circle the sequence words from page 49 that helped you.

Read through the list of materials you need to make a parachute.

How to Make a Parachute

Materials Needed:

string

scissors

ruler

napkin

cork

Now number these steps in order:

_____ Then tie one piece of string to each corner of the napkin.

_____ After tying the string to the napkin, tie the remaining four loose ends of the string to the cork.

_____ Finally, drop the parachute from a high place and watch it float down.

_____ Second, unfold a square paper napkin.

_____ First, cut four 10-inch pieces of string.

Go back and <u>underline</u> the words from page 49 that help you to put the steps in correct order.

Create Your Favorite Sandwich

Here is another example of a how-to paragraph.

How to Make My Favorite Sandwich
A list of ingredients I will need:
a veggie burger
a bagel
honey mustard
relish
a slice of onion
a piece of cheese

My favorite sandwich is a veggie burger on a bagel. This is how I make it. I need a veggie burger, a bagel, mustard, relish, a slice of onion, and cheese. First, I set out the bagel. Next, I cook the veggie burger in the microwave and put it on the bottom half of the bagel. After that, I spread mustard and relish on the burger. Then, I add an onion slice and a piece of cheese. After that, I put the sandwich into the microwave to melt the cheese. Finally, I put the top half of the bagel on the sandwich. Now I can eat. Yum!

Go back and (circle) the organizing words in the sandwich paragraph.

✎ Exercise

Now it is your turn to create your favorite sandwich.
First make a list of ingredients you want to have in your sandwich. Be as creative as you wish—it doesn't have to be a real sandwich!

_____   _____

_____   _____

_____   _____

Now write a paragraph describing how to make your sandwich. Look at the list of organizing words on page 49 for ideas on how to help you put your paragraph in the best order.

My favorite sandwich is really the best! This is how I make it. First,

_____

_____

_____

_____

_____

_____

_____

_____

_____

_____

Getting Ready

Here is another how-to paragraph for you to read.

How to Prepare for a Hike

My Planning List:

1. check the weather
2. pack all these things
   in my backpack:
   - map and compass
   - T-shirt and shorts
   - socks and sneakers
   - sun protection (hat, sunglasses, sunscreen)
   - sweatshirt
   - water bottle and snack

Begin by writing a topic sentence.

Topic sentence: *Each time I hike, I learn a little more about what to bring to be well prepared.*

Notice the paragraph begins with a topic sentence. The topic sentence is followed by details including the items from the planning list.

How to Prepare for a Hike

   Each time I hike, I learn a little more about how to be well-prepared. First, I check the weather. Comfort is most important. If it is going to be warm, I usually wear a cotton T-shirt and gym shorts. I am very careful to pull my socks on smoothly before I put on my sneakers to prevent blisters. Next, I always put on sunscreen, sunglasses, and a hat to protect me from sunburn. Then I pack water and a snack in my backpack. It's also important to bring a map and a compass if you are unfamiliar with the area. Finally, I stick in a sweatshirt just in case it gets cool. A day hike is much more fun when you are well-prepared.

Notice that the author explains *why* or *how* the items were used. Does the concluding sentence sum up the paragraph on page 54?

☐ yes   ☐ no

✎ Exercise

Now work with a partner to plan your own how-to paragraph. First fill out your planning list, then write a topic sentence.

How to Study for a Spelling Test

Our Planning List:

_____

_____

_____

_____

_____

_____

Look at your list on page 55. Write your topic sentence here:

_____

_____

Using the planning list you and your partner just wrote, write your own paragraph about how to study for a spelling test. Remember to use the sequence words on page 49 to help.

Begin with your topic sentence. Don't forget to indent!

_____

_____

_____

_____

_____

_____

_____

_____

_____

Now read your paragraph to your partner.

Paragraph Checklist

When you write a paragraph, you can use this checklist to make sure you haven't forgotten anything important.

- ☐ Do you have a topic sentence?

- ☐ Do you have at least two or three good detail sentences about the topic?

- ☐ Did you indent your first sentence?

- ☐ Did you use capital letters at the beginning of each sentence? Names of people and specific places? Titles?

- ☐ Did you use punctuation at the end of each sentence?

- ☐ Did you write a good conclusion?

- ☐ Is your handwriting clear and easy to read?

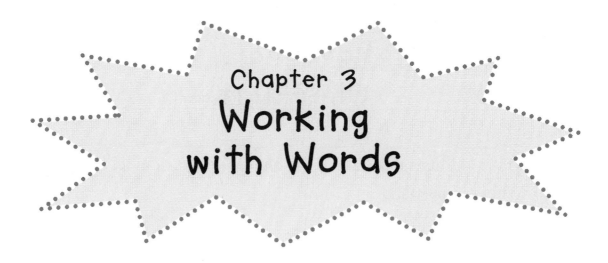

Try to choose interesting and exciting words when you are writing. Your writing will be more clear and enjoyable to read.

Overused Words

The words *like* and *said* get used a lot. After a while, it gets boring for your reader. Your writing will be more interesting if you stop using the words *like* and *said* and instead tell *why* you like something or *how* someone said something.

Like

Here are two different ways to avoid using the word *like:*

1. Start the sentence with a new subject.

    Example:

    Boring sentence: I like my coach.

    Interesting sentence: My coach makes soccer practice really fun.

2. Start the sentence with descriptive words about your topic

    Example:

    Boring sentence: I like ice cream.

    Interesting sentence: Delicious, sweet, ice cream is one of my favorite treats.

✎ Practice

Now you try. Change these sentences by using one of the ways explained on page 58.
Look at the synonym list on page 162 for words you can use instead of *like*.

1. I like pizza.

_____

2. I like to read.

_____

3. I like video games.

_____

4. I like my teacher.

_____

5. I like recess.

_____

6. I like to ride my bike.

_____

7. I like playing baseball.

_____

8. I like sneakers.

_____

When you use many sentences with *like* in a row, things get boring for your reader. Look at these paragraphs. The assignment is to write a paragraph about spring.

Brainstorming list
flowers
baseball
rollerblading
biking
not wearing coats

Paragraph #1

I like the beautiful flowers. I like to play baseball. I like going rollerblading. I like riding my bike. I like it when it is warm enough so we don't have to wear coats.

Paragraph #2

Spring is my favorite time of the year. The early spring flowers are colorful and smell so sweet. I get excited when my baseball coach calls to tell me the practice schedule. On days when we don't have practice, my friends and I rollerblade or ride bikes. It is great when it is warm enough to leave our jackets at home.

Give two ways these paragraphs are different.

_____

_____

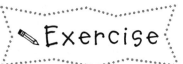

✎ Exercise

Get a partner and brainstorm about summer. What does summer make you think of? Make a list on the next page.

What does summer make you think of?

_____

_____

_____

_____

_____

_____

Use your list to write a paragraph about summer. Do not use the word _like_.

_____

_____

_____

_____

_____

_____

_____

Now read your paragraph to your partner.

Said

Said is another overused word. This paragraph is an example of using the word *said* too much.

My Uncle Ralph <u>said</u> that he was upset about the new building in town. He <u>said</u> he was concerned about the environment. He <u>said</u> that sometimes when they build they destroy land where animals live.

The next paragraph shows how you can use more interesting words instead of said. Notice how the new words give more information about how Uncle Ralph feels:

Uncle Ralph <u>grumbled</u> about a new building in town. He <u>complained</u> that he was concerned about the environment. Sometimes, he <u>explained</u>, new buildings require destroying lands where animals may live.

• Practice

Read the following sentences and then choose a verb to replace the underlined word(s). (Circle) the verb that you think fits the best.

1. He <u>said in a big voice,</u> "Stop talking right now!"

   (asked, demanded, pleaded)

2. I <u>said</u>, "Come quickly!"

   (sang, hollered, muttered)

3. "Look at the huge fish I caught!" her mother <u>said</u>.

   (whispered, exclaimed, replied)

4. "Was the test easy?" <u>said</u> Ian.

   (laughed, asked, called)

5. "I don't feel very well," Emma <u>said</u>.

   (grumbled, shouted, giggled)

6. "But I don't want to go to bed!" Tyler <u>said in unpleasant voice</u>.

   (grinned, declared, whined)

Other Overused Words

Like and *said* are not the only words that can be boring to your reader. You should always try to use lively and interesting verbs when you write. Read each sentence below. Choose a better verb to replace the underlined one in the sentence.

• Practice

1. Feeling tired, the old man <u>went</u> home.
   (flew, staggered, crawled)

2. The wet, hungry puppy <u>barked</u> to come inside.
   (sang, yelped, howled)

3. After winning the game, Philip <u>went</u> back to tell the news.
   (raced, flew, bounced)

4. The spaghetti sauce <u>went</u> down his shirt.
   (dribbled, jumped, trickled)

5. The military soldiers <u>went</u> in the parade.
   (strolled, hiked, marched)

6. The injured girl <u>called</u> to her father for help.
   (cried, yelled, whispered)

7. Pedro <u>likes</u> baseball. He plays it every afternoon.
   (enjoys, adores, prefers)

8. She <u>ate</u> her piece of birthday cake and asked for more.
   (gobbled up, tasted, consumed)

9. The eagle <u>flew</u> above. He was beautiful to watch.
   (soared, staggered, glided)

Write five of your own sentences using descriptive verbs and adjectives. Don't use *like, said, goes, nice, bad,* or *went.* If you need ideas for other words to use, look at the list of synonyms on page 162.

1. _____

2. _____

3. _____

4. _____

5. _____

Using Comparisons

When you want to describe something, it often helps to compare it to something else.

Read these examples:

She sings like a nightingale.

He's as watchful as a cat.

My baby sister's skin is soft as silk.

His sudden laugh was a volcanic explosion.

His bald head was as shiny as a bowling ball.

✎ Practice

Complete these sentences using interesting comparisons. Be creative!

1. Next to the elephant, I felt as small as

_____

2. He was as hungry as

_____

3. The library was as quiet as

_____

4. She was as pretty as

_____

5. The sudden scream was like

_____

6. He moves as carefully as

_____

7. I was so hot that afternoon that I felt like

_____

8. She snapped at me like

_____

9. The cemetery was

_____

10. His shadow was

_____

11. He ate his sandwich like

_____

✎Exercise

Now write your own paragraph that includes three creative comparisons. Be sure to indent the first sentence and use correct capitals and punctuation marks.

_____

_____

_____

_____

_____

_____

_____

_____

Chapter 4
Writing a Story

*I*t's time to put together everything you know about sentences and paragraphs and write a story.

As you are writing your stories, don't forget that there are resource materials at the back of the book that you might find helpful like story planners and checklists to make sure you didn't forget anything.

Story Planning

Before you write a story, it is a good idea to think of ideas and make a plan for what you want to write. Our minds are filled with good ideas, and brainstorming is a way to get them down on paper in a simple way. Don't think about whether the idea is good or bad before you write it down. Just write!

Once you have some ideas down on paper, you can choose which idea you like best. Then you can think of what you want to write about your idea. The idea you choose for your story is called the **topic.**

Listing

Making a list will help you remember the topics you think of while you are brainstorming.

For example, here is a list of possible ideas you could write about:

- a bear in our campsite
- my favorite game
- the scary storm
- a funny person

Now make a list of things you might want to write about. Just go ahead and write! You can decide later which idea you like best. If you run out of space for your ideas here, you can add more on page 161.

_____

_____

_____

_____

_____

_____

_____

_____

Starting Your Story

Now that you've come up with some topics, you're ready to start writing your story. A story needs to include certain elements. You may remember them from Book 1.

1. Story Planning
2. Characters
3. Feelings
4. Senses
5. Setting
6. Problem
7. Conclusion

The next few sections will focus on these elements.

Story Planning: Using a Web

A web is a good way to organize your brainstorming. The web below shows an example using one of the topics from page 68, *a bear in our campsite*. Notice how the web organizes the details for the story.

we gather wood

bear looking for food

bear gets picnic basket

bear leaves with basket still stuck on his head

A Bear in Our Campsite

movement in campsite

we stay still

bear's head gets stuck in basket

we laugh all night

A story based on this web could look like this:

Monica and I were so excited to go camping. As soon as we got to the campsite, we set up the tent. It was getting late, so we decided to gather some wood for our campfire. As we were returning to the campsite we noticed something moving near our tent. When we stopped to get a better look, we realized it was a bear. He was looking for food, and we had left our picnic basket out in the open. We stayed very still, hoping he would not see us and leave. We didn't go near him because bears are dangerous. The bear started thrashing around and making noise. We could see that he had put his head in our picnic basket and it was stuck. Boy was he mad! Finally, he took off. He was crashing into trees and bushes and making a lot of noise since the basket was covering his eyes. At first we were very quiet when we got back to our campsite, then we just burst out laughing and could not stop. We knew we would not have any dinner that night, but we were laughing too hard to eat anyway.

✎Practice

Now pick one of your ideas from page 68. Write it on the web below and then brainstorm for details for your story.

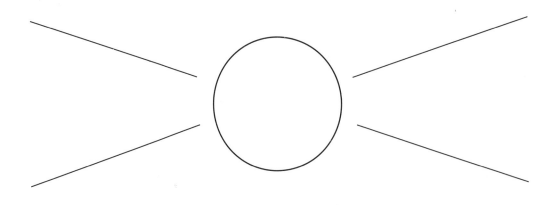

Exercise

Now write a short story below using the details from your web. Think about writing complete sentences with interesting verbs. Try to use at least one comparison.

_____

_____

_____

_____

_____

_____

_____

_____

_____

_____

_____

_____

Story Plan

Here is a different kind of web called a story plan. Words like *who, what, where, when, why,* and *how* can help you to come up with details about your topic.

Here is a sample plan.

A Scary Storm

Who? me and my family

What? bad weather report
—went to beach anyway

Where? near the beach

When? summer vacation

Why? had to leave beach,
storm approaching

How? ran to the train station

How does story end?

We were safe from the storm and decided to go to a movie.

The story could be something like this:

The weather channel reported that a stretch of bad weather could be heading our way. It was summer vacation and we wanted to go to the beach. The sky was a brilliant blue with no clouds in sight. We were a little worried but decided that maybe the storm would miss us. We packed up our stuff and took the train to the beach. When we got out at the station, we noticed that the sky to the north was quite dark. As we put down our towels, the dark sky was moving closer. As a matter of fact, we were quite surprised by how fast it was moving. We quickly packed up and headed back to the train station. As we were walking over the sand dune, there was a sudden loud crack of thunder. As we dashed to the station, it started to rain and blow very hard. Just as we got inside, we heard hail make loud plunking noises on the roof. As we stood on the covered platform, we felt very lucky that the station was so close to the beach. Mom suggested that we go to the movies when we got home. We all thought that was a great idea.

•Practice

Now you plan a story using the webs below, and the words *who, what, where, when, why,* and *how* to help you plan. You don't have to use all of the question words. Only use the words that are helpful to you. You may use one of your topics from your list on page 68 or make up a new one.

How does the story end?_____

_____

_____

Write a short story using the details from your web. Your story should also include more details than just those on the web. The notes on the web are just a beginning.

_____

_____

_____

_____

_____

_____

_____

_____

_____

_____

_____

_____

Characters

Characters are people or animals that are important to the story. When planning a story, one of the steps is to create interesting characters.

There can be more than one character in a story, but usually there is one that is the most important, or the **main character.**

When writing your story, be sure to give the reader details about how the characters look and what they are thinking. These kinds of details make your characters seem real.

Animal Characters

It is fun to write about animal characters. Read the list of physical (or outside) features about an animal character below:

- tall
- long neck
- long legs
- spotted coat
- short tail
- deer-like head

Did you guess what my animal is? Read the description below to find out.

Gregory is a tall giraffe who lives in Africa. He has a very long neck and a rather round body with long skinny legs. His tail is short with a tuft of fur at the end. His elongated neck allows him to eat leaves off the tops of trees. His lofty, spotted body makes him look awkward, but he is actually quite graceful when he walks.

• Practice

From this description, draw a picture of Gregory below.

How can we describe the personality of an animal character? We can generally tell
a lot about an animal by the way it acts.

Here are some words that could describe the personality of an animal.

gentle	mean	curious
funny	clumsy	fast
smart	dangerous	wild

• Practice

Choose a word from the list above that means the same as a word below and write it on the line.

awkward _____

quick _____

wise _____

silly _____

When you describe an animal character, you need to think about what the animal looks like and what kind of personality it has. This paragraph describes both what this character looks like and his personality.

Leon thought he was the coolest lion in the jungle. He was one of the largest cats and he knew it. He was very proud of his thick yellow fur coat and bushy mane. When he woke up each day, he would strut down to the river to brush his coat. Then he would admire his reflection in the water. He loved the way his round ears stood up tall in front of his bushy mane. He would inspect his piercing yellow eyes and strong square jaw and stroke his little white beard. He would think to himself, "I am truly the best looking lion in the jungle, and no one can compare!" He would then look around to see who was watching and let out a giant roar just to scare any animals nearby. As he settled down for a nap in the warm sun, he would chuckle, thinking about how handsome and strong he was.

• Practice

Circle the words that describe Leon:

shy   fun

proud   self-centered

kind   vain

mean   bully

                    thoughtless

From the details given, draw a picture of Leon

Exercise

Now it's your turn to make up an animal character. First picture your animal character clearly in your mind.

List three words that show what your animal looks like.

1. _____

2. _____

3. _____

List three words that describe its personality.

1. _____

2. _____

3. _____

Now write a paragraph using the list above to describe your animal character. Be sure to use correct, complete sentences.

_____

_____

_____

_____

Ask a friend to use your description to draw a picture of your animal character on a separate piece of paper. See if it is close to the picture you had in your mind.

Human Characters

It is also fun to describe human characters. Read about the physical features of this imaginary person.

girl named Melinda

fourth-grader

long, black curly hair

likes to dress up

big brown eyes

smiles a lot

Melinda is a very tall fourth grader. She has long black hair that curls in lots of different directions. Melinda loves getting dressed up. She always wears bright earrings that shine through her hair, and she likes to wear the color red. Melinda has big brown eyes, and she is always smiling.

•Practice

From this description, draw a picture of Melinda.

Now it is your turn to make up a **person.** First, picture him or her clearly in your mind. List words that describe what your character looks like or, if you prefer, make a web.

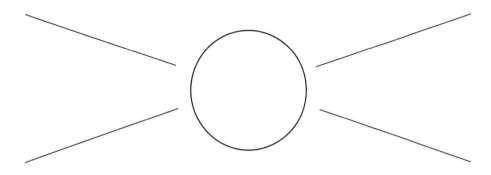

Write a paragraph using the web above to describe your person. Be sure to use correct, complete sentences.

_____

_____

_____

_____

_____

_____

_____

How can we describe someone's personality and what they're like inside?

The way a person acts tells a lot about him or her. What can you tell about a person who is . . .

quiet?   selfish?

kind?   jealous?

sad?   shy?

thoughtful?   funny?

                  cheerful?

Think about what kinds of things people do to show their personality.

How does a friendly person act?

_____

_____

_____

How would you know a shy person?

_____

_____

_____

Imagine a character, then draw a picture to show what your character looks like. Write your character's name under the box.

Name: _____

Now list 2 words that describe your character's personality, and explain how your character shows this part of his or her personality.

For example:

<u>Funny</u> = <u>Everyone bursts out laughing each time Bob makes a face.</u>

_____ = _____

_____ = _____

When you write about a character, it is important to *tell* and *show* what their personality is like. For example, if you just said that someone was funny without explaining what you meant, it would not tell us enough.

Write a sentence to explain these different parts of someone's personality.

Example:

careful

Tamara always counts her change at the store to make

sure it's correct.

1. selfish

_____

_____

2. grumpy

_____

_____

3. thoughtful

_____

_____

Exercise 3

Describing Zack

Read the following paragraph and see if you can tell what type of personality Zack has.

Zack arrived at school yesterday in a nasty mood. He said that his older sister was mad at him because he would not share his new scooter. "Why should I share my beautiful, new scooter with my sister?" he wondered. Then, at recess, he said that he wouldn't play ball unless he could be the pitcher. When Ms. Teffy told him that he had to take turns, Zack got grouchy and marched off. Another time, Zack brought a new book on whales to show the class but wouldn't let anyone look at the book or the pictures. He would only show the cover. Jeff and Tim were good friends with Zack, but ever since he took their cupcakes, they haven't wanted to be around him. I don't blame them.

Name four details that tell you about Zack's personality.

1. _____

2. _____

3. _____

4. _____

When you describe a person, there are lots of details to think about.

Read this paragraph and notice the details.

Mrs. Angleroot is our new neighbor. She is very tall and plump. She wears great big glasses and dresses in old-fashioned clothes. Her skirts are long and she wears a big hat every day. Mrs. Angleroot always smiles and is very friendly. Whenever she sees me, she says "Hello" and lets me pat her dog. Yesterday, she reminded me that Halloween is soon and that she is going to have lots of treats for my friends and me. This morning, she offered to bring my mom some soup and wondered if we might like to taste one of her fresh apple pies. In the evening, I love to hear her playing the piano. I think we are lucky to have Mrs. Angleroot as a neighbor.

What details tell you about Mrs. Angleroot's personality?

_____   _____

_____   _____

_____   _____

List a few words that describe what Mrs. Angleroot looks like.

_____   _____

_____   _____

_____   _____

From the details given, draw a picture of Mrs. Angleroot.

Writing about Someone Special

Before you write about someone, you need to gather some information. One way to do this is to ask questions about that person. Think about someone who is special to you and answer the following questions about that person.

1. What is the person's name?

_____

2. How old is he or she?

_____

3. Where is he or she from?

_____

4. How long have you know each other?

_____

5. What does he or she look like?

_____

_____

6. What are at least two or three words that describe your special person's personality (what he or she is like)? If you're having a hard time thinking of adjectives, look at the list on page 92.

_____

_____

7. What do you like to do together?

_____

_____

_____

_____

8. What is one time that was very special with this person?

_____

_____

_____

_____

9. Why is this person important to you?

_____

_____

_____

_____

Here are some adjectives that could describe a special person.

helpful	musical
patient	smart
considerate	intelligent
kind	clever
gentle	strong
understanding	forgiving
thoughtful	curious
sympathetic	shy
funny	quiet
easygoing	brave
cheerful	courageous
fun	proud
playful	fearless
friendly	daring
talented	tough
athletic	determined
artistic	strict

Pick two or three of the adjectives you chose to describe your special person. Write a sentence that tells why each word describes your special person.

Word 1: _____

_____

_____

_____

Word 2: _____

_____

_____

_____

Word 3: _____

_____

_____

_____

Before writing your paragraph, decide what information you want to use from your notes. Make a list or use the web below. The choice is yours.

_____

_____

_____

_____

_____

_____

or

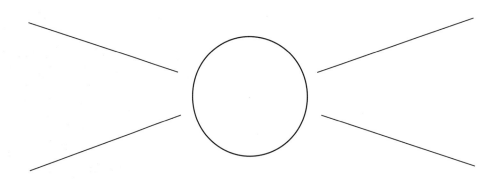

✎Exercise, part 3

Now write a paragraph about your special person. Use the notes you first gathered. Include the words you chose to describe your special person and explain why you chose these details to describe this special person.

Remember: indent your paragraph and use correct punctuation and capitals.

_____

_____

_____

_____

_____

_____

_____

_____

_____

_____

_____

_____

_____

_____

_____

_____

_____

_____

_____

Content Editing

Read through your paragraph.

- ☐ Did you make a plan by gathering facts about our special person before you started to write?

- ☐ Did you use your notes to help you write your paragraph?

- ☐ Did you describe what your special person looks like?

- ☐ Did you use at least two or three adjectives to describe your special person?

- ☐ Did you explain why each of these words help to describe your special person?

- ☐ Did you read over your paragraph to be sure what you wrote makes sense?

- ☐ Is your handwriting clear and easy to read?

Dialogue

A good way to give information about your characters is to have them talk to each other. The way people talk can tell you a lot about their personality. When the characters in your story talk to each other it is called **dialogue.** Dialogue adds variety to your writing.

Read what Jerry and Matt are saying.

What kind of personalities do you think they have?

Hey, Jerry,
I really like your drawing.
I didn't know you were
such an artist.

Thanks, Matt,
yours is good too.
I love how you draw people.
They look so real.

Circle the word that best describe Matt's and Jerry's personalities:

shy   rude

thoughtful   grumpy

Now read this dialogue between Ben and Jess.

Ben, you're
making us late!

Too bad, Jess.
I can't leave without my books.
Besides, we're usually early.

If we're late,
you're to blame!

Circle the best word or words that describe Jess.

generous   impatient

nervous   gloomy

Often, the way someone talks can even give you an idea of their age.

Read the dialogue below. Who do you think is speaking? Draw a picture of each character.

Please, pretty please, let's go see the ponies. Can't we go now? I really want to go now. Please! Come on!

Stop begging. Just be patient. I told you we would go later this afternoon.

Which person did you decide is older?

_____

Quotation Marks

Look at the dialogue below.

Bill asked, "Mark, would you like a lift to work?"
Mark replied, "Yes! I just missed my bus. Thanks!"

Notice how the words that are spoken are framed by **quotation marks.** Whenever someone is speaking in your story, you need to put quotation marks around their words. Check to make sure that your quotation marks are put in front of the first word that is spoken and at the end of the last work that is spoken. And remember: whenever a new person speaks, you need to start on a new line.

Practice

Now, rewrite the sentences below. Add quotation marks at the beginning and at the end.

1. Will you come to my party on Sunday?

_____

2. Wow, what a game!

_____

3. Where were you yesterday?

_____

✎ Exercise 1

Read the conversation between Mara and Alice:

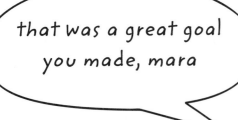

Now rewrite the dialogue between Mara and Alice on the lines below. Be sure to use quotation marks and capital letters where appropriate. Remember that each speaker needs a new line.

_____

_____

_____

_____

Now read this conversation between Chris and his dad:

dad, is it time to go to mario's house

not yet chris put your things away first

Write the conversation between Chris and his father on the lines given below. Remember: each speaker needs a new line. Don't forget capital letters and quotation marks!

_____

_____

_____

✎ Exercise 2

Put quotation marks and capital letters in the following sentences.

1. let's go to the zoo! justin called out.

2. jenny asked, do you want to go trick or treating with me?

3. pack up your bags, our counselor said.

4. what happened? asked miss allen.

5. toby exclaimed, we drove to tampa to see the game!

Read the examples below. Notice how the words people say are framed by quotation marks. Think about what you learn about the characters' personalities from their conversation.

1. "Granny, what are you looking for?" asked Ruthie.

   "My glasses, sweetie. I lost my glasses again."

   "I'll help you, Granny. Let's look in the kitchen."

What did you learn about Ruthie's personality from that dialogue?

_____

_____

2. "Move out of my way! Let me through!"

   "Stop talking that way, Leo, and don't shove!"

   "Move! Didn't you hear me?"

What did you learn about Leo's personality from that dialogue?

_____

_____

3. "Be sure to stretch before you leave," said Coach Bartlett.

   "But my friends are waiting for me!" said Kelly.

   "It was a long game, Kelly. If you don't stretch you could injure your muscles,"
   explained the coach.

Do you think the coach is being mean or careful?

_____

_____

✎ Exercise 4, part 1

With a partner, imagine two very different characters.

First decide what type of personality each character has, and think about their interests. Use the web below to brainstorm for ideas. Use one web for each person. Write the character's name on the line below the web.

My partner is _____

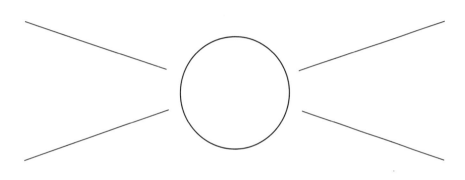

Name: _____

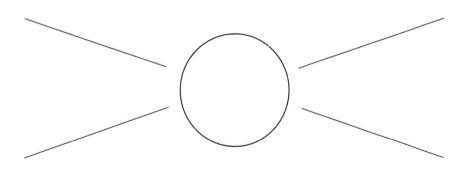

Name: _____

Using your webs for ideas, write a few good sentences describing each character. You can write about one character, and your partner can write about the other.

_____

_____

_____

_____

Read your descriptions aloud when you are finished.

✎ Exercise 4, part 2

Now think about how each person might show their personality and interests when they speak. With your partner, decide what the conversation will be. Practice the conversation as if you and your partner were in a play. Then write it below using proper punctuation marks.

Remember that each time a new person speaks, start a new line.

_____

_____

_____

_____

_____

⟶

_____

_____

_____

_____

_____

Now have fun reading your conversations to the class.

Editing Checklist

You can use this checklist to help you make fewer mistakes in your paragraphs and stories. Read through the conversation you wrote on the previous page and check things off if you did them.

☐ Did you use a capital letter at the beginning of each sentence? For names and titles?

☐ Is there the correct punctuation at the end of each sentence?

☐ Did each speaker start on a new line?

☐ Did you put quotation marks around what each person says?

☐ Did you use complete sentences?

☐ Did you use descriptive adjectives and a variety of verbs?

☐ Is your handwriting clear and easy to read?

Writing from a Different Point of View

It's fun to imagine what life would be like if you were someone or something else. Try to put yourself in someone else's shoes and imagine what would be different.

✎ Practice

Here are some ideas about how different life might be from another point of view. Work with a friend and add some more of your own.

1. If I were a school principal . . .

   I would be sure to get to school on time.

   I would try to learn the names of all the students.

   _____

   _____

   _____

2. If I were an ant . . .

   Everything would seem huge.

   I might be afraid of being squished.

   _____

   _____

   _____

   _____

3. If I were a fish living in a fish bowl . . .
   I might swim along the top looking for food.

_____

_____

4. If I were eighty-five years old . . .
   I might need a cane.

_____

_____

5. If I were a bird . . .
   I would love hopping from tree to tree.

_____

_____

_____

6. If I were a ball . . .

_____

_____

_____

_____

Pick what you would like to pretend to be and write a paragraph. You can use an idea from the practice exercise or you can make up our own. After you have finished your paragraph and proofread it, exchange it with a partner. Have fun sharing your paragraphs.

Read this example before you begin. It is from the point of view of a spider.

> Help! Some careless person just walked into my web. Oh dear. I was so afraid of that. However, I see that the flies that I caught are still there. They are going to be food for my babies. I must repair my web and make sure that nothing is damaged. Those flies are heavy to move around, but maybe I can get help.

I will write from the point of view of _____

_____

_____

_____

_____

_____

_____

_____

Feelings

Your characters have feelings. A character that shows feelings will seem real. When you write, try to have your characters show feelings about what is happening to them or around them.

• Practice

Read this story. Think about how the main character feels.

The Big Trip

Sophia has been counting the days until she leaves San Francisco to go see her grandparents in Monterey, California. She is nervous about going on a trip on the bus all by herself, without any of her sisters or brothers, but at the same time, she is excited because she loves her grandparents and wants to see more of California.

As the departure day comes closer, however, Sophia starts to feel tense and gloomy. Her stomach is a little upset. She tells her mom that she thinks she is sick. Sophia's mom realizes that Sophia might be feeling panicked because she has never traveled by herself before. She asks Sophia if she would be happier if Anna, Sophia's older sister, goes with her to Monterey. Sophia said, "Yes, that would be great!" Sophia's mom calls Sophia's grandparents to ask if they mind if Anna visits, too. The grandparents are pleased. Sophia and Anna cheerfully pack their things and get ready to leave. They giggle with excitement.

✎ Practice

1. In the first paragraph, how does Sophia feel about going to California?

_____

_____

_____

2. How do her feelings change at the beginning of the second paragraph?

_____

_____

_____

3. How does Sophia feel at the end?

_____

_____

_____

Go back and <u>underline</u> the words that show feeling.

Read this story and fill in the blanks with words that show Ben's feelings. You may use the words below or choose your own. Do not use a word more than once.

embarrassed	afraid	shocked
excited	miserable	impatient
lonely	scared	nervous
lucky	eager	worried
relieved	astonished	thrilled

Ben's Uncle Mark is a fisherman off the coast of Maine. Ben wanted to go out fishing with his uncle. One day Ben became _____ and pleaded, "Will you take me out to check the lobsters? Will you take me out to catch tuna? Please, please take me with you!"

Finally, Uncle Mark phoned Ben to ask him to come out the next morning. Ben was _____ and said "Yes! I'll be there." However, when he heard that he had to be on the boat by 4:00 A.M., Ben was _____. He knew that he had a very hard time getting up early. He started to feel _____ about being ready on time. His mom found him a very loud alarm clock. This _____ him. That night he was so _____ that he hardly slept at all. When the alarm went off, Ben was already

awake. He jumped into his clothes and ran to the dock, but was

_____ to discover how dark and cold it was outside. He

felt _____ that he was dressed in shorts and a T-shirt,

but his uncle just laughed and loaned him a heavy jacket. Later in the

morning, the sun came up and warmed everything. At that point, Ben

and his uncle were tired and had plenty of lobsters to bring back home.

Ben felt _____ that he was there.

Reactions

When something happens in a story, the characters have a reaction or a feeling
about it.

Look at the example of the web below:

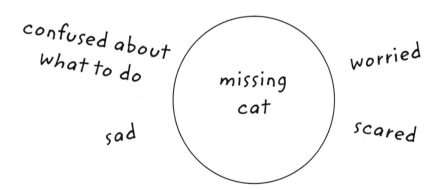

In this story idea, the cat is missing. The character feels confused about what to do
about her missing cat. The character also feels sad, worried, and scared. These
feelings help you realize how upset the character is and how much she cares for her
cat. This makes the story seem real.

Here are three webs with situations that could happen in a story. Write at least three ways the character might be feeling on each web. You may refer to the list of feelings on page 112 for ideas.

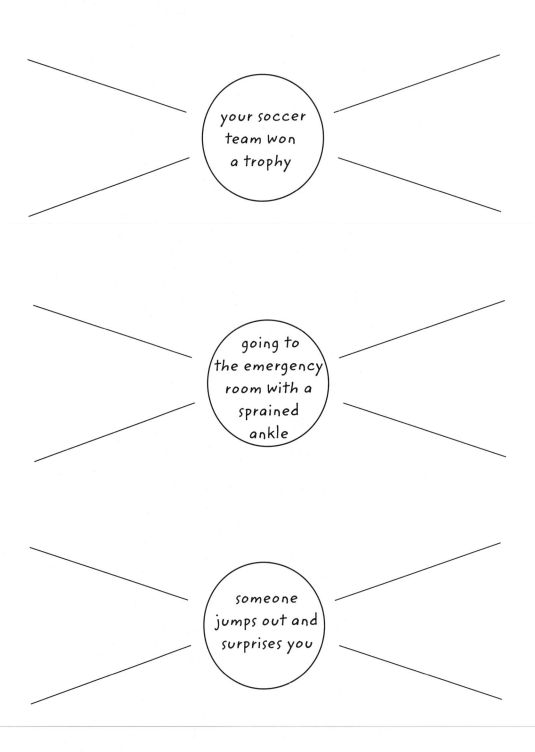

Changing Feelings

Read the following story and notice how the narrator's feelings change. Also, notice how the author makes paragraph breaks to show a time change or a change in subject matter.

My tooth was bothering me. It had been loose for weeks. On Thursday, it finally came out during gym class. The gym teacher sent me to the nurse, who wrapped the tooth carefully in soft paper and sent me back to class.

Later when I got home, I proudly showed my tooth to my big sister and Aunt Millie. They were happy to see it because they were tired of seeing it wiggling around in my mouth. They told me to put the tooth under my pillow. I did, and then I forgot about it until much later.

That night, I remember lying in bed thinking about what my friend and I would do on Saturday. Then I must have drifted off to sleep. I was suddenly awakened when I heard the door to my bedroom open. There was a creaking sound and then steps coming into my room. The footsteps came closer and closer! My heart started beating so fast I thought it would burst. It felt like screaming, but I was too scared. I kept my eyes closed hoping that what ever was in my room would disappear. I lay motionless with my eyes shut tight. The footsteps stopped at the edge of the bed. Frozen with fear, I stayed under the quilt. At last, the steps tiptoed back to the door, which quietly closed. My panic was over. I slid up from under the covers and began to relax.

Guess what! In the morning while stretching, my hand brushed against a brand new dollar bill under the pillow. Wow! I remembered my tooth and pictured the tooth fairy sneaking into my room. I could not help laughing at myself when I remembered how scared I had been during the night. I cheerfully jumped out of bed to show everyone what I had found.

✎ Practice

Underline the words and phrases (groups of words) that show how the character in the story on page 115 is feeling.

How did the narrator's feelings change? How did he feel at first and then how did he feel at the end?

_____

_____

_____

_____

Now go back and notice the paragraph breaks. There are three different paragraphs. What do the breaks in the paragraphs show?

_____

_____

_____

✏ Exercise

Make up a short story to describe how these children are feeling. Why do they have the expressions they do on their faces? Who are they? Where are they? What happened? You may want to use a web to brainstorm on a separate sheet of paper before you start writing.

You can have the characters' feelings change somewhere in the story. If you do, remember to start a new paragraph to help your reader understand that a change is taking place.

Here are a list of words that describe feelings.

surprised	worried	confused
comforted	excited	relieved
annoyed	happy	unhappy
overjoyed	astonished	frustrated
shocked	miserable	silly
impatient	sorry	determined
irritated	scared	terrified
delighted		sad

_____

_____

_____

_____→

_____

_____

_____

_____

_____

_____

_____

(Circle) the words on page 117 that describe the children in your story.

Senses

Writing can be more interesting when you use your five senses.

seeing

smelling

hearing

touching

tasting

• Practice

Which of the five senses best describes these phrases? Write in your choice. You may want to select more than one.

1. hot, buttery popcorn ___smelling_____

2. a fluffy bunny _____

3. a painting _____

4. week-old garbage _____

5. a rock concert _____

6. spring rain _____

7. a fresh cut lemon _____

8. sandpaper _____

9. low tide _____

10. a dripping faucet _____

11. an icy wind _____

12. warm brownies _____

✎ Exercise 1

Fill in the sense or senses that go with the ideas listed below. Some may have more than one. The first has been done.

1. getting into a hot bath tub _touching_____

2. beautiful field of tall grass _____

3. a crying baby _____

4. a skunk _____

5. a patch of spongy moss _____

6. a marching band _____

7. chocolate sauce on ice cream _____

8. the howling wind _____

9. a shiny, red car _____

10. a turkey roasting in the oven _____

11. a door slamming shut _____

Write a sentence of your own describing a particular sound.

_____

_____

Write a sentence of your own describing a particular taste.

_____

_____

How can you use your five senses to describe a beach? Here are some ideas:

salty water	dead fish
colorful sail boats	crying sea gulls
kids playing	Frisbees
pounding waves	fishing boat
bright sun	hot sand
refreshment stands	fog horn
slimy seaweed	ocean spray
suntan lotion	bumpy barnacles

Circle the ideas that have to do with feelings.

Underline the ideas that have to do with hearing.

Write down three things that you can see but not smell.

_____

Write down two things that you can smell.

_____

✎ Exercise 3

Notice how different senses make you think of different describing words for water.

touch: *cool* water

hearing: *rushing* water

smell: *polluted* water

sight: *blue* water

taste: *salty* water

Fill in a word in these sentences that describes the sense indicated.

Touch

1. The _____ grass tickled my toes.

Smell

2. I cracked open a _____ rotten egg.

Taste

3. I needed a drink of water after I ate those _____ peanuts.

Sight

4. We knew it would be a good day when we saw the _____ sky.

Hearing

5. You could tell by the _____ voices that something exciting had happened.

Exercise 4

Work with a partner. Each person should draw a picture of a zoo. Include many different things you might see, hear, smell, taste, and feel at the zoo.

Now exchange pictures with your partner. In the categories below, list as many sense words from your partner's picture as you can.

See

_____

_____

_____

_____

_____

Taste

_____

_____

_____

_____

Feel

_____

_____

_____

_____

Hear

_____

_____

_____

_____

Smell

_____

_____

_____

_____

Setting

The **setting** for a story is like a set for a play. When the curtain opens on a stage, you see scenery that shows you something about the setting. When you begin reading a story or a book, there usually is some description telling you when and where the story takes place.

• Practice

Think about the setting in the following paragraph. Look for words that will give clues about the time of day and the weather.

> Suzy sits on her stoop next to her empty glass of lemonade. Drops of sweat dribble down the side of her face. She wants to take off her shoes, but she knows the pavement would be too hot for bare feet. She looks up, squinting in the sunlight, and watches a bird soar high above the buildings. "If only I could fly like that," she thinks to herself, "and feel the wind on my face." Suzy sighs and wipes her forehead. Her older sister, Shanda, opens the door.
>
> "Hey Suzy," she calls, "want to cool off?"
>
> "You bet I do," Suzy groans, "what can we do?"
>
> "Follow me," says Shanda, handing her a towel. "We can go to the fountain in the park!"

What is the weather like? _____

Underline the words that are clues about the weather.

Where do you think this story takes place? _____

As you read this paragraph, notice the details that let you know where and when the story takes place. Notice the details that set the scene.

Even though my mom was with me, walking home was really scary. It was dark and spooky. The air felt thick, as if there were electricity in it. Only a few streetlights were working. All the others had gone out, so the buildings and stores were black. Every few minutes, thunder crashed and gusts of wind blew in our faces. We ran for home. Just as we reached our block, a streak of lightning blazed across the sky and lit up the street. We raced up the steps and opened the door just as the rain poured down.

When is the story taking place? _____

Where does the story take place? _____

List details that help to describe the weather.

_____

_____

_____

_____

_____

When you describe your setting, you need to be sure that you use words that fit. Read the words below and write them on the line under the correct setting.

seagulls

ocean

dry

cactus

waves breaking

swimmers

vultures

fish

camels

lizards

seashore   **desert**

_____   _____

_____   _____

_____   _____

_____   _____

_____   _____

Look at this web that describes the scene of a fire. What do you see? Add any details that are missing to the blank lines on the web and draw a picture in the box.

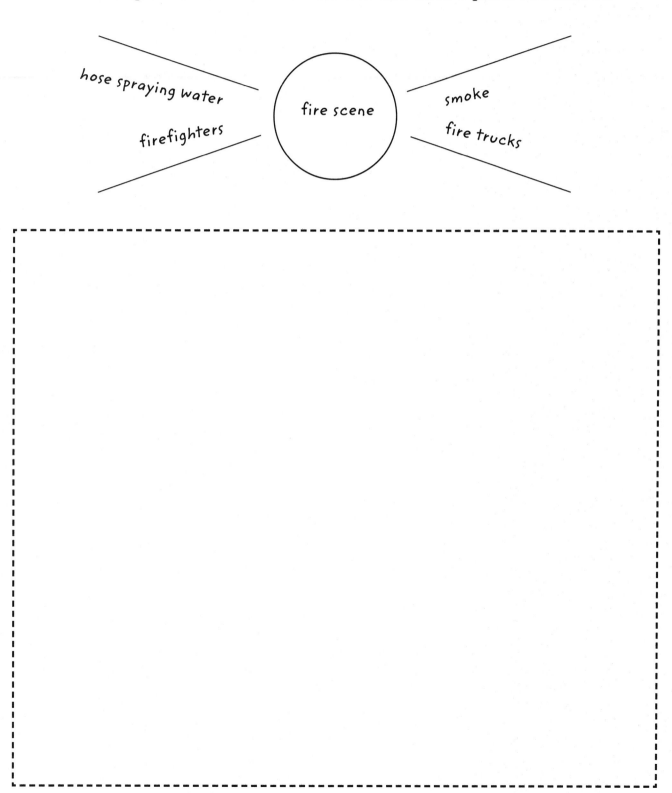

Write a short paragraph describing the scene you just drew on page 129 of the fire. Don't forget to include details from the web.

_____

_____

_____

_____

_____

_____

_____

_____

Write four or five sentences describing a place at a certain time of year. Instead of just naming the place, use details. Describe the time of day, but don't say if it is morning, midday, or night; just use clues.

_____

_____

_____

_____

_____

_____

_____

_____

Read your paragraph carefully to yourself, and then exchange it with a partner. Ask your partner when and where the story takes place, and at what time of day.

Editing Checklist

Reread your last writing piece. Use this list to make sure that your paragraph is the best that it can be.

- ☐ Is there a capital letter at the beginning of each sentence?

- ☐ Is there punctuation at the end of each sentence?

- ☐ Did you indent the first line of your paragraph?

- ☐ Did you use complete sentences?

- ☐ Did you use descriptive adjectives and a variety of verbs?

- ☐ Is your handwriting clear and easy to read?

Problem

A story often has a problem. The problem could be as simple as Henry losing his lunch box or as complex as aliens invading from another planet. Sometimes the most exciting adventure stories have to do with just one person struggling against the natural elements such as a snow storm or a flood. The problem captures your interest while you read. You want to know what is going to happen.

✎ Practice

Add a problem to the following situations:

The first one is done for you.

Situation	Problem
Pedro's friends are starting a bike club.	<u>Pedro does not see well</u> <u>enough to ride a bike.</u>
Iris has her science fair tomorrow.	
Calvin is meeting Max to skateboard.	
A squirrel is carrying a cheekful of nuts to store for the winter.	
Alana is baking cookies.	

Situation	**Problem**
The hockey team got new uniforms.	_____
	_____
Mrs. Picklepepper packs a lunch box for her grandson to take on his field trip.	_____
	_____
Michael takes his daughter, Sabine, fishing.	_____
	_____
Kara and Sophie decided to explore their attic.	_____
	_____
I woke up early and peeked out the door to discover two feet of powdery snow.	_____
	_____

Situation	Problem
Last Saturday our swim team had their championship match.	_____ _____
Luis's family wants to leave Mexico and move to Oklahoma.	_____ _____

✎ Exercise

Look at this example that describes two events that happen because of Pedro's problem.

Problem _Pedro does not see well enough to ride a bike._

_____

Event 1 _Pedro tells his friends that he wants to be part of the bike club, but first he needs to go to the ophthalmologist to see if he needs glasses._

Event 2 _Pedro goes to the doctor. He gives Pedro prescriptive sports glasses._

Now pick two problems from pages 132–134 and make up two events that happen because of each of them.

Problem. _____

_____

Event 1 _____

_____

_____

Event 2 _____

_____

_____

Problem. _____

_____

Event 1 _____

_____

_____

Event 2 _____

_____

_____

Story Mountains

Now we will go back to the situation of Pedro. We will put the events of the story on this **story mountain.** Story mountains are another way to plan a story. They make it easier to follow the action of the story clearly. Story mountains help you pay attention to the sequence of the events and how the story builds.

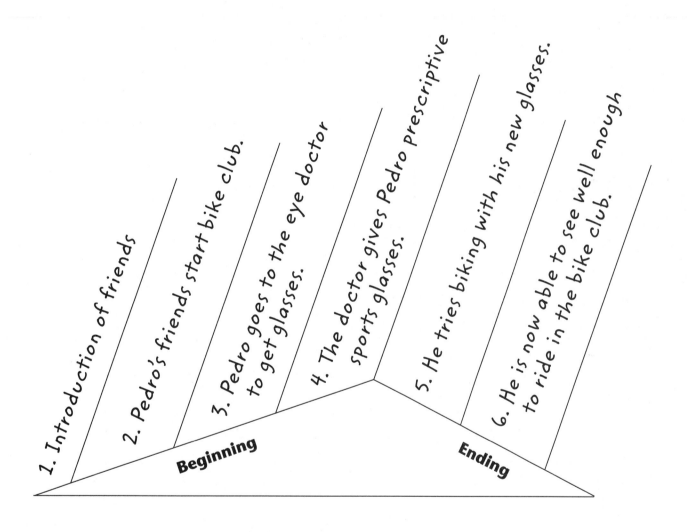

1. Introduction of friends
2. Pedro's friends start bike club.
3. Pedro goes to the eye doctor to get glasses.
4. The doctor gives Pedro prescriptive sports glasses.
5. He tries biking with his new glasses.
6. He is now able to see well enough to ride in the bike club.

Beginning

Ending

Problem: _Pedro can't see well enough to ride a bike._

See how the mountain is like a timeline? You read it from left to right. The events on the left happen first. They move up the line to the peak, which is the **turning point.** From there, they move down to the end of the story.

You may find that your stories are easier to write when you use a story mountain. **Remember** that you will need to expand upon each event to make each part of the story real. For example, the story about Pedro might go something like this:

Pedro has three best friends. Jake is ten years old just like Pedro. They have been in the same class for three years. Fred is a year older. He lives in the building next door, and he loves to play outside and ride his bike. Meredith is also ten, and she loves riding her bike too. She goes to the same neighborhood park as the boys.

One day when they were over at Fred's place, Pedro's friends told him that they all wanted to start a bike club. Pedro was sad because he was afraid that he would not be able to ride a bike the way his friends can. Pedro didn't see very well. For a long time he couldn't figure out why he couldn't do some things as well as his friends. He hesitatingly told his friends that he wasn't sure if he could join the club. Later in the week, his mom took him to an eye doctor. The doctor gave him prescriptive sports glasses.

When he got home he put on his bike helmet and new glasses. Even though he was a little nervous, he tested out his new glasses by riding his bike up and down the sidewalk. He was excited that he could see really well and bike riding was such fun! He quickly called his friends and told them that he could join the club after all.

The next Saturday, he met his friends at Meredith's house. They all cheered when they saw Pedro arrive with his bike. Everyone grabbed their helmets and hopped on their bikes. The bike club was finally complete, and they rode off.

Now it is your turn. Choose one of the situations from the previous pages, or exchange a situation and problem with a partner. Write the problem on the line below the map; then put the events on the story mountain.

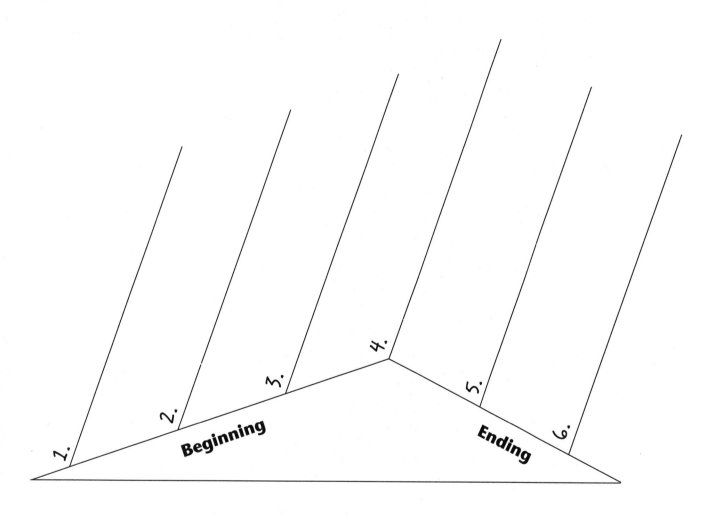

Problem: _____

_____

_____

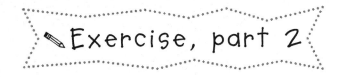

Exercise, part 2

Congratulations! You are ready to write a longer story.

Using your map from the preceding page, write your story. Remember to expand where you can and to include interesting details.

_____

_____

_____

_____

_____

_____

_____

_____

_____

_____

_____

Conclusion

A story needs an ending. The reader likes to know what happens to the characters and if their problems get solved. The ending is also called the **conclusion.**

✎Practice

Look back at the story about Pedro and the bicycle club. What is the conclusion of that story?

_____

_____

_____

Exercise

Now you will have the chance to add your own conclusion to two stories.

Read the following stories and then add on your own conclusion. When you are finished, read your complete stories to a partner and compare your conclusions.

It was a clear Sunday afternoon. Tim and I packed our lunch, which we planned to take over to the baseball field. We wanted to practice pitching and hitting, and then eat our sandwiches under a tree in the shade. However, the plan changed because Tim had to take care of his sister while his mom went to the store. We took her to the park with us, and she ate her sandwich with us under a tree. Then she started begging us to play ball with her. The trouble was she couldn't hit anything because the bat was almost as big as she was, and she couldn't catch anything either. She got really frustrated and started to cry.

_____

_____

_____

_____

_____

Jimmy felt miserable. The third-grade class was going on a field trip. His teacher had asked everyone to bring a lunch in a paper bag, but Jimmy had forgotten to bring his lunch. He couldn't call home, because his parents were at work. Claire said that she would share half of her sandwich with him, but it was peanut butter and jelly. Jimmy hated peanut butter.

_____

_____

_____

_____

_____

_____

_____

Story Maps

Here is one more way to plan a story. The notes are all filled in except for the conclusion. Write some notes of your own for a conclusion, then turn to the next page and finish writing the story.

Topic: _A Hiking Trip_ _____ **Author:**_____

Characters:

Janet and Jessica

Setting:

a mountain in Utah

Problem:

They get lost.

Action 1:

They take a shortcut.

Action 2:

They go into the wooded area.

Conclusion:

✎ Practice

Now add a conclusion to the story about Sally and Jessica

     Sally and Jessica were hiking up a mountain in Utah. When it came time to come down, they decided to take a shortcut. Jessica had done this before with her father. The shortcut meant going into the woods and climbing through some rough areas until they got back to the trail. When the girls got into the woods, they realized they had no idea where they were.

_____

_____

_____

_____

_____

_____

_____

Read your story to a partner. How are your conclusions different?

_____

_____

Now fill in your own story map. You can brainstorm for a topic on a separate sheet of paper or use one of the story starters on page 161 to give you an idea.

Topic: _____ Author: _____

Characters:

Setting:

Problem:

Action 1:

Action 2:

Conclusion:

Exercise, part 2

Write a story based on your map on page 147.

_____

_____

_____

_____

_____

_____

_____

_____

_____

_____

_____

_____

Chapter 5
Editing and Publishing

After you have written a story, it is a good idea to read it again to see how you can make it even better. When it is as good as you can make it, you can turn the story into a book by adding a cover and pictures.

The first step is to choose one of the stories you have written in this book. This is the one you will publish. Find the story that you think is the most interesting or the one that was the most fun to write.

Finalizing the Content

The second step is to make sure the content makes sense. At this point, you just want to make sure you have not left anything out, and that the events in your story are in a logical order.

A good way to check your story's content is to read it out loud. Listen to yourself as you read and make sure what you have written is clear. Your ears often pick up what your eyes don't see!

Remember: don't worry yet about punctuation, spelling, or capital letters.

Content Checklist

Read the story you have chosen again. Then look at the items in this checklist. You don't always have to include everything, but use this list as a guide to help make sure your story is the best it can be.

- ☐ Does your story have a clear topic?

- ☐ Does the sequence of the story make sense?

- ☐ Have you included at least two or three interesting details about your characters?

- ☐ Did you show your characters' feelings about what is happening?

- ☐ Did you include dialogue?

- ☐ Did you tell where or when the story took place?

- ☐ Do your characters have to deal with a problem?

- ☐ Did you include any of the five senses?

- ☐ Did you make good word choices?

- ☐ Did you use any comparisons?

- ☐ Do you have an interesting conclusion to your story?

✎ Practice

Using the same story as in the checklist on page 150, answer the following questions.

1.Where does your story take place?_____

_____

2. In what time of the year or at what time of day does your story take place?

_____

_____

3. Write two or three interesting details about each of your characters.

_____

_____

4. What feelings do your characters show?

_____

_____

5. What is the main idea of your story?

_____

_____

_____

6. What are some details you have used to support the main idea?

_____

_____

7. What senses did you use in your story?

_____

_____

8. Is the conclusion happy, sad, or another emotion?

_____

_____

Editing

The next step is to check your punctuation and capital letters to make sure you have used them correctly. Check the spelling of any words that you think you might have spelled wrong. Use classroom resources such as dictionaries and textbooks, or ask your teacher for help. It's a good idea to keep a list of words you use often in your writing. Then you can just look at your list when you're not sure how to spell a word.

Editing Checklist

- ☐ Did you use a capital letter at the beginning of each sentence? For names and titles?

- ☐ Is there the correct punctuation at the end of each sentence?

- ☐ Did you indent your paragraphs?

- ☐ Did you use complete sentences?

- ☐ Did you put quotation marks around what each person says?

- ☐ Did each speaker start on a new line?

- ☐ Is your handwriting clear and easy to read?

- ☐ Did you correct or underline misspelled words?

On the page that has your story, mark any changes you need to make. Try to write neatly so that you can still read your story easily after you make the changes. Be sure you've added all the new words you want to include. Fix your spelling, punctuation, and capitals if you need to. Then read your story out loud again. Make sure your new changes make sense.

•Practice

Now swap stories with a classmate. Use the checklist on page 153 to see if you've missed any mistakes.

Choosing a Title

If you haven't already given your story a title, now is the time. Some writers like to wait until they are finished writing a story before they think of the title. Others like to think of a title first and then write the story. Either way is fine.

If you are having trouble thinking of a title, ask yourself some questions about your story.

Who is the main character in my story?_____

_____

What happens to this character?_____

_____

Is there an event or idea that is the most important thing in the story?

_____

_____

_____

Try to think of creative titles for your stories. If you are stuck, don't be afraid to give your story a simple title. Then change it later if you think of a better one.

Publishing

It's fun to publish a story by making it into a real book. You can add illustrations, include an "About the Author" page and make a colorful cover.

You need to follow several steps to publish your story.

1. Choose one of your favorite stories from the ones you have written.

2. Complete the Content Checklist on page 150.

3. Complete the Editing Checklist on page 153.

4. Write the changes you need to make on your story page.

5. Write a final draft of your story. This means that you will rewrite your story on a separate piece of paper and include all the changes and corrections you have made. Use your best handwriting or type it on the computer so your story is easy to read.

6. Write some facts about yourself on the "About the Author" form (page 156) and use that form to write a paragraph about yourself. Include that paragraph with your story. If you want, draw a picture of yourself or paste a photo on that page.

7. Make your cover. You can use crayons, markers, glitter, colored paper, or any other supplies in your classroom. Add a line to the cover that says, "Written and illustrated by. . . "

8. Staple your book together, or tie the pages and cover together with yarn or string.

Now your book is ready to share with your classmates, friends, and family.

Congratulations!

About the Author

Fill out the form below. Then use it to plan an "About the Author" paragraph that you will include in your published book. (You can include other information about yourself, too). Write your paragraph on a separate piece of paper and place it at the end of your book.

Name _____

Your age _____

Where you live _____

Where you go to school _____

What you like to do in your free time _____

_____

Your favorite things to write about _____

_____

_____

Chapter 6
Resource Materials

We have included 4 different planning sheets to help you brainstorm and organize your stories. You might find that you like one organizer better than the others. There is also a list of story starters for you to consult and a glossary of writing words for you to consult.

Story Web

Put your story idea on the line in the center of the web and then brainstorm for details about your story.

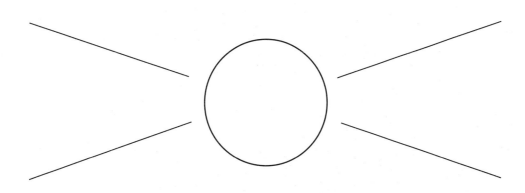

Story Plan

Use the words *who, what, where, when, why,* and *how* to help you plan your story.

Topic: _____

Who?

What?

Where?

When?

Why?

How?

How does the story end?_____

_____

Story Mountain

Write the problem on the line below the story planner; then put the events of the story on the story mountain.

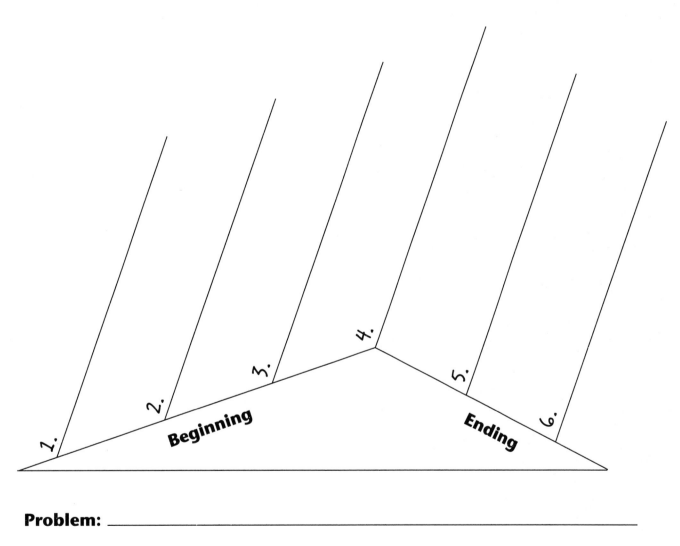

Problem: _____

_____

_____

Story Map

Topic: _____ Author: _____

Characters:

Setting:

Problem:

Action 1:

Action 2:

Conclusion:

Story Starters

1. I found the weirdest thing in my pocket, but then I remembered how it got there.

2. Did you hear what happened when Alice went camping?

3. When my Aunt Tanya takes me out in the stroller, I usually see lots of things going on...

4. An alien has come to our town. He (or she) is very strange.

5. The first thing that happened when the lightning struck was...

6. He ran when he heard Andrea crying...

7. Mars is a wonderful place to live...

8. Life as a tadpole is very difficult...

9. I always wanted to join the circus...

10. I took an exciting ride in a hot air balloon...

Here is a space to write some of your own starters.

_____

_____

_____

_____

_____

Synonyms

Synonyms are words that mean the same thing or almost the same thing. You can use synonyms to add variety to your writing. Here are synonyms for some words that you will often need to use in your writing.

bad: terrible, horrible, difficult, nervous, sad, boring, nasty, awful, evil, mean, naughty, spoiled, gloomy, discouraging

big: bulky, colossal, enormous, gigantic, great, immense, large, massive, substantial, vast

fun: enjoyable, entertaining, good time, joy, pleasure, treat, amusing

good: acceptable, excellent, great, positive, superior, valuable, capable, expert, satisfactory, useful, well-behaved, fantastic

got: acquired, borrowed, bought, received, achieved, earned, fetched, gained,

happy: joyful, glad, cheerful, contented, delighted, ecstatic, elated, gratified, merry, overjoyed, pleased, thrilled

like #1: adore, enjoy, love, admire, appreciate, approve

like #2: alike, similar, identical, resemble, same

nice: friendly, fun, cute, silly, thoughtful, adorable, amazing, great, wonderful, exciting, kind, charming, pleasant, agreeable, polite, cheerful

ran: bolted, darted, chased, hurried, jogged, raced, rushed, scurried, escaped, fled, proceeded, galloped

sad: depressed, blue, dismal, down, gloomy, glum, mournful, somber, unhappy, wistful, miserable

said: declared, whispered, asked, screamed, hollered, yelled, explained, shouted, replied, commented, grumbled, nagged, demanded, pleaded, exclaimed, continued, complained, inquired, laughed, yawned, grinned, growled, called, boomed, gushed, whined, questioned

went: left, departed, moved, passed, set off, travel, proceeded

Glossary

adjective: a word that describes a noun

adverb: a word that describes a verb

character: a person or animal in a story

conclusion: the last part of a paragraph or story

dialogue: a conversation between two or more people in a story

fragment: an incomplete sentence

indent: to start the first line of a paragraph in from the edge of the page

main character: the most important character in a story

noun: a person, place, thing, or idea

paragraph: three or more sentences about the same subject

predicate: the part of a sentence that describes what happens to the subject

quotation marks: the punctuation marks used at the beginning and ending of what someone says in a story

setting: the background of the action in a story; where and when a story takes place

story mountain: a way to plan a story that looks like a mountain

subject: 1. the person or thing being discussed in a paragraph

2. the person or thing that a sentence is about

supporting sentence: a sentence in a paragraph that describes the topic

synonyms: words that mean the same thing or almost the same thing

topic: what a paragraph or story is about

turning point: an important event in a story that solves the problem and leads to the conclusion

topic sentence: the sentence in a paragraph that explains what the paragraph is about

verb: an action word